Professo

Presents Car

Author: L

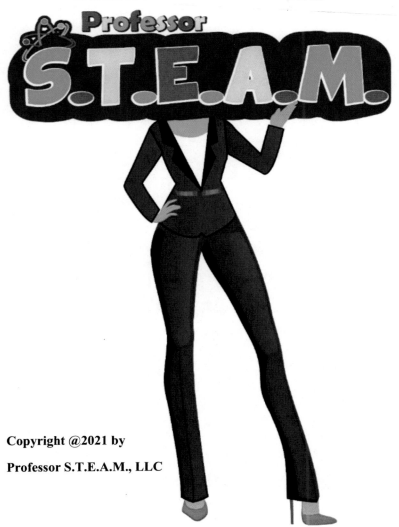

Dedication

This book is dedicated to every girl and boy who has a dream and to supportive adults who are there to inspire them.

DREAMers are S.T.E.A.M.-ers

Special thanks to my sensational seven; my mother Carolyne, brother Edgar, sister Kimberly, son Michael Jr., daughter Kadence, and two inspirational coaches, Dr. Martin Stewart and Dr. Cruz-Craig, who encouraged me to pursue my dreams.

Have you ever thought about the future - what will exist and what will be?

Professor S.T.E.A.M. brings exciting opportunities for you and for me.

So, let us take a trip
to see what exists
and what will be.

I want you to see
how S.T.E.A.M. will
shape our world
with creativity.

Our first stop is **Science**, it is exploring our world using measurements at different locations.

It is learning about our world using data, research, and observation.

The next stop
is
Technology,
it is
developing
something
new.

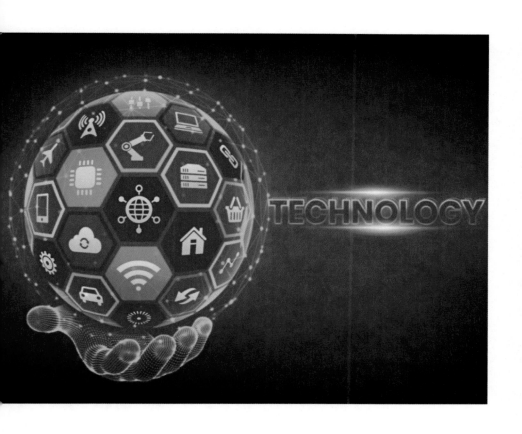

Like software products and services that can tell you what is false and what is true.

The third stop is Engineering- these careers design buildings, bridges, cars and planes.

It's constructing something new by using your brain.

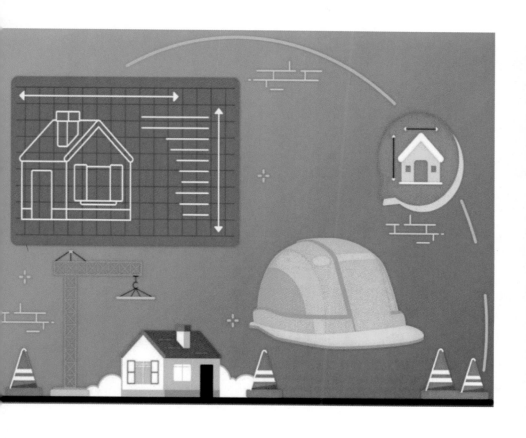

Math is the fourth stop, which uses logic, numbers, and shapes.

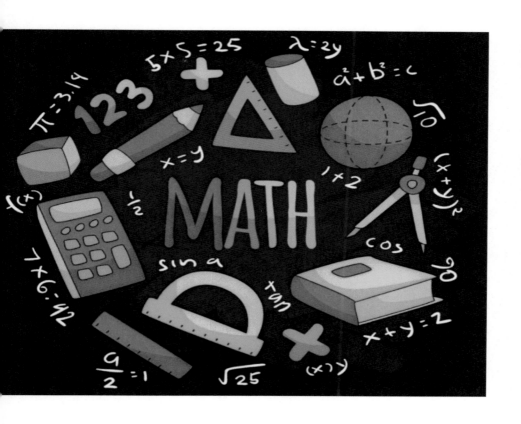

Math counts, measures, and describes everything around us in each and every place.

We discussed S, T, E, and M hooray! Can you tell me what letter needs to be added to make S.T.E.A.M. complete today?

A stands for Arts and plays a role in S.T.E.A.M. in a very important way.

No trip would
be complete
without using
pictures,
colors, and
prose.

29

Art is dancing, singing, and crafting as we draw this trip to a close.

Professor
S.T.E.A.M.

will show you the future, you can do anything to set your mind to do.

Science,
Technology,
Engineering,
Arts,
and Math,
will create endless
opportunities for
you.

Key Terms:

Science – a creative way to organize, discover and create

Technology – methods and processes to deliver products and services using devices

Engineering - designing and building structures like bridges, roads, and machines

Arts – creatively communicating through colors, sculptures, singing and dancing

Math – using logic, numbers, and geometry to develop patterns

Visit
www.ProfessorSTEAM.org
for more educational
resources

PROFESSOR STEAM

PROF_STEAM

PROFESSORSTEAM

PROFESSOR S.T.E.A.M.

Professor S.T.E.A.M.

About the Author

Professor S.T.E.A.M. is the brainchild of Dr. Kandis Boyd, PMP. She is a S.T.E.A.M expert, with nearly 30 years of hands-on experience in science, technology, engineering, arts, and math. Dr. Boyd has been a motivator, mentor, and a manager throughout her career and has served as a strategic S.T.E.A.M communicator for emerging endeavors. She  is a global speaker, renown expert, and has written over 50 articles and hosted over 30 podcasts on S.T.E.A.M. topics. Dr. Boyd is a Professor and has taught students of all ages for over a decade.

The Professor S.T.E.A.M. series is a culmination of her two passions - teaching youth and S.T.E.A.M. activities. This rhyming storybook is intended to introduce S.T.E.A.M. concepts to tomorrow's leaders in a fun and engaging manner.

 Dr. Boyd is the recipient of the 2018 American Public University's Graduate Teaching Excellence Award, and the Office of Oceanic and Atmospheric Research's 2019 Equal Employment Opportunity (EEO)/Diversity Individual Award. Dr. Boyd is also the 2020 winner of the American Meteorological Society's Charles E. Anderson Award for Diversity, Equity, and Inclusion, the 2020 Recipient of the Black Engineers of the Year (BEYA) Award for Career Achievement, and the 2020 Recipient of the National Weather Association Special Achievement Award for Lifetime Achievement.

Made in the USA
Middletown, DE
09 March 2023

26455478R00022